Wilber Allen Campbell

Judas Iscariot

Or, Kings and Traitors

Wilber Allen Campbell

Judas Iscariot
Or, Kings and Traitors

ISBN/EAN: 9783337307929

Printed in Europe, USA, Canada, Australia, Japan

Cover: Foto ©ninafisch / pixelio.de

More available books at **www.hansebooks.com**

JUDAS ISCARIOT;

...OR...

KINGS AND TRAITORS.

❧

A LECTURE

—— BY ——

REV. WILBER ALLEN CAMPBELL.

❧

PRESS OF CURTS & JENNINGS,
CHICAGO, 1897.

JUDAS ISCARIOT;

— OR —

KINGS AND TRAITORS.

✤ ✤ ✤

In opening this lecture I will present for your study brief biographical pictures of the three traitors of history: Benedict Arnold, the Duke of Marlborough, and Judas Iscariot.

Shakespeare tells us that

"The evil that men do lives after them,
The good is oft interred with their bones."

But I have noticed that that depends largely upon which they do last. A doer of good may at the last day of his life by one fell stroke overturn the good deeds of a lifetime. While a doer of evil may on his last day, in penitence and repenitance, recompense fourfold the evil deeds of a lifetime.

It is difficult to conceive of darker, blacker crimes than those committed by King David: adultery, perfidy, murder! And all from the vilest motives. Yet the heart that plotted murder, and the ruin of Bathsheba afterwards repented in sackcloth and ashes; and the hand that killed, and that crucified virtue afterwards gathered the gold and the silver for the Temple, and indited the Psalms; and the heart of David became so tender and affectionate that he would gladly have died for the unnatural Absalom.

Not so Benedict Arnold. The good which he had done was smothered by the venomous breath of treachery; and the fair name which he had won for himself was by his own hand exchanged for a traitor's pottage.

It has been truly said that Benedict Arnold was as brave a man as ever lived. It was but the turn of a die that made him "Arnold the traitor" instead of "Arnold the patriot." But it was his own hand that turned that die. Benedict Arnold saw the ladder of fame stoop to take him upon its shoulders; he saw the gilded chariot of honor pause at his threshold to invite him to its purple seat; and he gazed upon the laurel wreath of victory which a new nation was about to place upon his brow. But the ladder of fame he spurned; and the chariot of honor he challenged; and the laurel wreath of victory he brushed aside, to see it afterwards exchanged for a crown of guilt.

This man was so great a lover of independence that he gave his private fortune of seventy-five thousand dollars to equip the American army of the Revolution. More than that, he offered his life-blood upon the altar of American independence. He was one of the first in the field; he led his troops like a king; he fought like a demon; he charged at Ticonderoga and Crown Point, and by his matchless manœuvering they fell; he took St. Johns; Washington selected him from among all his generals and sent him across the trackless jungles of Maine to take Quebec. His army waded through sloughs of despond, and carried the army impedimenta hundreds of miles, in the dead of winter, over rough quarries, rocks, hills and precipices, and never halted until Quebec was reached. And on all of that lonely march Arnold was not in the rear, but in the lead. Their food became exhausted; starvation stared them in the face; the hour arrived when the last ration was to be measured out, an ounce of pork to each man, which ounce of pork was to sustain life only until the morrow, when, with the mocking kisses of the morning sun, that stalwart army was to fall upon its face and die in the pangs of hunger and starvation. Then it was that Benedict Arnold rose to his loftiest manhood, and dividing his own ounce of pork with two of his soldiers, he commanded them to keep their faces westward; and rising to the full stature of a conqueror, he shouted:

8

"On to Quebec! Washington and America!" and he safely led his troops into camp at the Canadian fort.

When Washington bowed his head in anguish, bereft of hope, it was Benedict Arnold who lifted up his arms, and who held his head above the drowning waters of despair.

But alas for Arnold! On a single night he quenched his spark of hope that shined so brightly; he heaped upon his victories the ignominy of a revenge so black, that it mocks the color of the starless night; and those dearly won titles, "Victor," "Hero," "Conqueror," he exchanged for a cross of infamy, with the superscription: "Traitor!" On that fateful night, when America was sleeping peacefully, and entrusting her liberty and her wives and her children to his safe-keeping, Benedict Arnold stooped himself into the shriveled Mr. Hyde, and whispered to the red-coat spy: "Here are the keys to West Point." And when Mr. Hyde got through with him he kicked him over onto English soil, where he died a few years later, pennyless and without a friend.

Those last sad years in London were years of self-reproach and bitter remorse. The iron frame which had withstood so many battles and weary marches through the wilderness at last broke down under the torture of lost friendships and merited disgrace. And now, as, broken in spirit and weary of life, he felt the last sad hour coming on, his mind kept reverting to his friend and lover, Washington— Washington, who stayed by the ship and she never went down!—and he called for his American uniform, and he put it on; and he decorated himself in those epaulettes and swordknots which Washington had given him after his victory at Saratoga.

He was in a rude, cold garret. I have read that an old, gray-haired divine kneeled at his side. It was his death hour.

"Would you die in the faith of a Christian?" faltered the minister, kneeling upon the damp floor.

The white lips of the death-stricken sufferer moved. He struggled to a sitting posture: "Christian?" he echoed. "Will it give me back my honor? Come with me, old man, come with me far over the waters. Ah, we are there! This is my native town. Yonder is the green where I sported when but a boy; yonder the church where I knelt at my mother's knee. But another flag waves yonder than the flag when I was a child. Listen, old man: Were I to pass along those streets as I passed when but a boy, the very babes in the cradles would raise their tiny hands and curse me; the graves in yonder churchyard would shrink from my footstep; and yonder flag would rain a baptism of blood upon my head. Faith? Will it give me back my honor?" Then his mind wandered. "Hist! Silence along the lines there, silence along the lines! Not a word, on the peril of your lives! Hark you, we will meet them, Montgomery, in the center of the town; we will meet them there, in victory or death. Now, on my boys, now on! Now, now, one more blow and Quebec is ours! On, on! Faith of a Christian? Will it give me back my honor?"

And himself tottering to an old chest he took from it an old American flag, tattered with the shots of the enemy, and spotted with the reddest, hottest blood of American independence; and winding the stars and stripes about him, he said: "Let me die in the uniform in which I fought my battles; may God forgive me for ever putting on any other!" And thus died Benedict Arnold, the traitor.

"Oh that our own true Washington had been there to sever that good right arm from the corse, while the dishonored body rotted in the dust; to bring home that noble arm and embalm it among the holiest memories of the past. For that right arm struck many a gallant blow for freedom: Yonder at Quebec, at Champlain and Saratoga, Crown Point and Ticonderoga. That arm, yonder beneath the snow-white mountains in the deep silence of the river of the dead, first raised into light the banner of the stars."

___

The Duke of Marlborough. There have been few characters so conspicuous in history as the untutored John Churchill, afterwards Duke of Marlborough. This man, because of his great military genius, long found apologists among the English historians, and many admirers among the common people, who paid the penalty for his advancement. But a bare recital of living facts convicts him of numerous treasons committed under the most aggravated circumstances of ingratitude. His whole life is one panorama of crime and treachery.

John Churchill began life as page to the Duke of York; the Duke of York became King James II. John Churchill delivered his own virtuous, innocent sister to be debauched as mistress and harlot to the King! Churchill received in exchange, estates and titles of nobility. Then, when the open follies of King James began to threaten the legs of his own throne, Churchill with his own hand struck those legs the fatal blow; and stealing the King's army went over into the field of the enemy, the Prince of Orange. Then, when the Prince of Orange had rewarded his perfidy with an earldom, the vile treachery of Churchill led him to betray his second benefactor, and he essayed to go back to the exiled James. He went instead to the tower of London. But unfortunately he was released; and a few years afterward he died, a model nobleman of the English peerage, upon the summit of political patronage.

Marlborough was a personal favorite; but secretly he was a *roue*. Marlborough was a statesman, but he was a robber. Marlborough was a hero, but he was a traitor! And the titled blood of Blenheim castle to this day is tainted and spotted with the unforgiven sins of crime and treachery, and the barter of estates and titles for the unpardonable sacrifice of a sister's virtue.

The third picture which I present for your study is that of Judas Iscariot, who sold his Lord for thirty pieces of silver.

Jesus and the twelve disciples became a permanent society, wandering and ministering up and down through Palestine and Perea; and as they received many contributions from the public, which they in turn gave to the poor, a treasurer became a necessity. So Judas, possibly because of his fitness for the position, or possibly because of his solicitation, was made treasurer. Then, having access to the treasury, it was but a question of time when Judas was to become a miser, an embezzler, a traitor.

At Bethany he laments the anointing with oil of the feet of Jesus by Mary who loved him. He said: 'Why this needless waste? This ointment might have been sold for 300 pence, and the money given to the poor." But we see that the canker worm had already begun to gnaw at the heart of Judas in the one simple line of comment of the Apostle: " Now Judas had the bag and was a thief."

During the last week in the life of Jesus, Judas seems to have concealed from the disciples his treachery. He goes with Jesus and the disciples every morning to Jerusalem and back again to Bethany at night. He looks upon the acted parable of the withered fig tree, and pretends not to know that himself is that withered fig tree; under a mask he talks confidentially with his Master; and he shares the vigils in Gethsemane. The Last Supper is prepared; Judas is at the table; he still would have them believe him faithful; his feet, with the feet of the rest of the disciples, are washed by the Master; he hears the fateful words: "Ye are clean, but not all; one of you shall betray me." One by one they ask: "Master, is it I? Is it I?" He too must ask or seem guilty; he has already sold his Lord for thirty pieces of silver, and has whetted the spear that is to pierce his tender heart; yet he dares to sit at his table, to dip from his dish and to insinuate honesty by asking: "Master, is it I?" He hears the condemnation: "What thou doest, do quickly." While sitting in the silence of pretended reverence the anxious heart of Judas is pumping to his fevered brain the blood of guilt; instead of feasting he is but counting the seconds when the cock shall crow that sounds the knell that summons him—not to heaven, but to hell. A paroxysm of guilt seizes him; he rushes from the chamber; with hair streaming and eyes glaring from their sockets he rushes down the by-path, under the trees, and emerges from the thicket into the open space which has long been the resort of the Savior, where await him his cohort of executioners. He whispers to the leader: "They come." And clutching the thirty pieces of silver in the trembling hand of a maniac, he paces wildly up and down the open space awaiting the oncoming of his friend and Master. Slowly, silently, mournfully he comes. Now, upon the action of Judas depends the destiny of a life; the destiny of a people; the destiny of a race; the destiny of a nation; the destiny of a world; the destiny of a soul. Look, look, see. Hiding the sweaty silver in the bosom of his gown, he rushes and with a lying ecstasy greets his Master with the fevered kiss of betrayal. Hark, listen! That kiss sounds to every corner of creation; it echoes against the rocks of the hills and the dome of the firmament; the celestial harps are silenced; the angels fall down at the feet of the mighty Omnipotent and implore arrest of this high treason; and in the throbbing silence of the great God, heaven and earth cry out: "It is finished, it is finished!" The Savior is led to the Praetorium, to Golgotha, to the cross, to death! And thus is paid the penalty for the sins of the world.

The innocent is led to the slaughter like a criminal; while the criminal sneaks away unpursued, yet chased by the conscious fires of hell, and the hate of those who bought his soul for thirty pieces of silver. Stung by remorse he goes and hurls the sweaty silver into the sanctuary, and quickened by the sight of the holy altar, he flies, crying:

"My conscience hath a thousand several tongues,
And every tongue brings in a several tale,
And every tale condemns me for a villian:
Perjury, perjury in the highest degree,
Murder, stern murder in the direst degree,
All several sins, all used in each degree,
Throng to the bar of justice crying all,
Guilty, guilty!"

And rushing forth he hangs himself; and, dying a suicide, he sees, in the thousand fantasies of a frenzied brain, his own ally, Satan, thrusting him through and through; and as the cursed steel comes back, he hears his fiendish: "Ha, ha! and if one spark of life be still remaining, down, down to hell, and say I sent thee thither."

And thus have passed into their graves the three traitors of history—three hissing serpents, three arrows of poison. In far-off India there grows a poison ivy; but wherever that ivy has grown, God, in his wisdom and in his love, has planted by the side of it an herb for antidote. So I have noticed that wherever in history there has grown up the poison ivy of treachery, God has raised up beside it the antidote of Truth and Kingship.

For Ahab and Jezebel, there was the Prophet Elijah.

For John Tetzel and Rome, there was Luther's thesis.

For the British at Orleans, there was a Joan of Arc.

For Napoleon Bonaparte, there was a Wellington and a Waterloo.

For English bigotry, there were the Pilgrim Fathers, who, with trembling hands, pushed their tiny barks out upon the stormy deep to plant the free church on the rock-bound coast of Massachusetts.

For Voltaire, there was a Whitefield.

For Benedict Arnold, there was a Washington.

And for Judas Iscariot there was—there is. there will always be—a Saul of Tarsus.

Now, I wish to show you that over against traitors and treachery there stand kings and kingship. The natural illustration is the kingship of David, the first great, true king of history.

When the children of Abraham entered the land of Canaan they found that kingdom without an organized government and without religon; consequently their occupation was warfare, and their practices were idolatry. This state of affairs continued over four hundred years. The Israelites were ruled by judges, prophets and priests. At length the Philistines preyed upon them and were about to consume them. They then petitioned their chief priest and prophet, Samuel, to give them an organized government, an organized army, and a king to lead them. Samuel heard them, and selected Saul, a brave, daring, brilliant young man, from the army. And Saul was anointed and crowned king of Israel; and the people rejoiced, and all seemed well. But Samuel at once had forebodings of the result. He saw in Saul crowned, a different man from Saul the citizen; he saw in Saul crowned, that ambition which makes men kill for glory, and which turns kings into despots. And his worst anticipations were fulfilled; for in ten short years Saul had run a course of sin and crime, and had rejected the Word of the Lord.

And the Lord sent Samuel to Saul, and he said to him: "Because thou hast rejected the Word of the Lord, therefore hath the Lord rejected thee from being king in Israel." And then and there was turned down one of the most courageous and brilliant young men of the whole army, who might have become the first king of sacred history; but he devastated his privileges, and turned his opportunities into crime, and in shame and disgrace he ended his life upon his own sword.

But the Lord had another king ready. He did not have to wait a single day. David, the shepherd boy, had already been anointed. But the only reputation he had, and the only stock he had in trade, was, that "David was ruddy, and withal of a beautiful countenance, and goodly to look to." But the Lord seeth not as man sees: "Man looketh upon the outward appearance; but the Lord looketh upon the heart." Although David still had his shepherd's crook in his hand, the Lord saw in his heart the stuff that kings are made of. And he was crowned King of Israel. And David was a king, both on the field of battle, and in the church of God. He started rightly. He accepted the Word of the Lord, which Saul had rejected. Those words—*accept, reject*—sound very much alike; but one led up to the throne of Grace; the other led down to the river of Death.

Contrasted with Saul, David was Hyperion to a satyr. He launched his reign as auspiciously as did Bolingbroke, when Richard II was forced to abdicate in his favor. Richard took the golden crown from his own head, and extending it to Bolingbroke he said :

"Now is this golden crown like a deep well
That owes two buckets, filling one another,
The emptier ever dancing in the air,
The other down, unseen, and full of water:
That bucket down, and full of grief, am I,
Drinking my tears, while you mount up on high."

And thus Saul sank, full of grief and drinking his tears, until, at last, he sank into a suicide's grave, cursed by God and unwept by man. While David mounted, and continued to mount, until at last, laying aside his Godly record beside his Psalms of praise, he mounted into the firmament of God, where awaited him a brighter, a perpetual crown of glory.

So much for the kingship of David. But I have noticed that there are other kings. There are still kings in Canaan. There are kings in America. There are kings for my auditors. For it is possible for every man, every boy, every girl and every woman to be a queen or a king. For, mark you, a king does not have to come from royal blood—he must come of loyal blood. A king does not have to be rocked in a cradle of ebony, nor fed from a golden spoon. He may come from the common people. In time of necessity he may be made.

To illustrate, I will relate to you a legend of ancient Abyssinia, to show how a king was once selected from the common people.

For many centuries, the legend recites, the empire of Abyssinia had been ruled by one dynasty, one line of kings. But now that dynasty was exhausted, there was but one remnant left—an old man now seated upon the throne, and childless. The people were ill at ease for the future king; for their superstition forbade them selecting a king from the common people. But the old king told them to be at rest, "For," said he, "when I shall have died I will return and rule you in spirit form." And by and by the old king died. And all went well for a time. But soon the land was involved in famine; the exchequer became exhausted; and brigands preyed upon the people. The king had forgotten to return in spirit form. Then the officers of the court called together the astrologers to have them consult the gods, whether a king should be selected from the common people. The astrologers deliberated, and then delivered the decree of the gods, that a king should be selected from the common people, and that the chamberlain of the court should select him. The chamberlain should go up and down throughout the empire, searching until he found the king, and this is the way he should know him. He is a man who is able to do three things which never man has yet accomplished: to feed the wild beasts from his hand; to produce fire by command; and to produce rain in time of drought—three things which man had never yet accomplished. The chamberlain hopefully started upon his quest. But after days and weeks and months of weary treading and searching, tired and sick at heart, he one evening turned into a rude hut in a recess of the mountain for food and shelter. There met him at the door an old, gray-haired man, who proved to be a philosopher. He was kindly fed by the old man. And as they sat by the hearthstone, in the darkness of the evening, the wild beasts of the forests came prowling and barking at the door of the hut, in hunger and ferocity. Without saying a word the old man reached to the roof of the hut, and taking from it pieces of dried meat, went to the door and fed the wild beasts from his hand. Upon arising in the morning the old man drew back a screen from the roof of the hut, and the sun shined through a peculiarly formed glass, and focusing its rays upon the hearthstone, the kindling burst into flame, and

the breakfast was prepared and eaten. After breakfast the old man led the chamberlain out into his
valley and showed him rich harvests of golden
grain and fruit and flower. And the courtier,
astonished, asked how he could have ripened grain
and fruit and flower when all the empire was in
famine. And the old man took him to the head of
the valley and showed him a great, natural reservoir
in the mountain filled with water; and where the
water would have escaped he had rolled a huge
boulder and the reservoir overflowed its banks and
the water, changed in its course, irrigated the valley.

The old man had fed the wild beasts from his
hand; he had produced fire by command; he had
produced rain in time of drought; the chamberlain
had found the king! Then he told him his quest
and at last persuaded him to return with him to the
court; and he was crowned and the empire was at
rest; the land was irrigated, the exchequer was re-
plenished and the brigands were expelled. And
when he died he decreed his successor from the
common people; and for many centuries the empire
of ancient Abyssinia was ruled by kings from the
common people, and had peace and prosperity.

The force of the illustration is plain : Kings do
not have to come from royal blood, but may in
time of necessity be made from the common people.

Then the question comes: What is a king?
A king is a man who can organize, who can
lead, who can control. And the chief requisite of a
king is that he be able to control himself. It is the
master-wheel in machinery which furnishes the
power; so it is the master-wheel that makes the
man; but it is the balance-wheel in machinery
which steadies the motion; so it is the balance-
wheel of judgment which makes the king. You
must be able to control yourself or you cannot control others; you must be able to practice your own
preaching—a difficult task. Portia said:

"If it were as easy to do as to know what were
good to do, chapels had been churches and poor
men's cottages princes' palaces. It is a good divine
that follows his own instructions: I can easier teach
twenty men what were good to do than to be one of
the twenty to follow mine own teaching."

Cardinal Wolsey very nicely taught his friend
and protege, Cromwell, how to be a king at court.
He said:

"Cromwell, I charge thee to fling away ambition!"

But, alas for the poor cardinal, he was unable to
practice his own preaching, and at the court of
Henry VIII. he fell, like Lucifer, never to hope
again.

Lady Anne stood before her subjects and publicly cursed the man who should shed innocent blood; and but a few weeks afterward Lady Anne was betrothed to Richard III., who killed her own husband.

Jesus said to Peter: "The cock shall not crow twice till thou shalt deny me thrice." And Peter answered: "Nay, Lord, though all men deny thee, yet will not I." And the loving, the hopeful, the impetuous Peter, who vowed eternal allegiance, in the twinkling of an eye forsook his Master and fled.

Rule thyself and then canst thou rule thy subjects. Napoleon Bonaparte learned to rule himself; then he successfully ruled his subjects and he became king of the second great empire. The Duke of Marlborough was doubly a traitor, false and treacherous to both James and the Prince of Orange; yet he could rule himself, and he retrieved the love of his countrymen which he had lost through treachery; and to this day it is the dead Duke of Marlborough who is king of England, and they decorate his false and faithless tomb every year in London. And but a year ago we patronized him, by selling to his descendant, the young duke, a homely American heiress and thirteen millions of money in exchange for his title and kinship—Marlborough the traitor!

But I do not censure a foreign lord for wanting to marry an American heiress. He has to have money, and as a general thing he has to have it right away—if he don't get it he can't keep his dukedom on straight. His proposition is a fair one. He says to the American heiress: "Money—nobility! Trade even?" And the girl answers: "Yes (te he!), and thank you, too." So he takes her millions—she goes along—and the first thing he does, with one million he rebuilds his great-granddam's rotten old palace; with the second million he establishes a fancy stable, don't you know, with fifty spavined, ring-boned, knock-kneed trotting horses, don't you know; then he entertains the other dukes once; plays the races once; gets drunk once; then he tells the pretty pale face that her clothes smell of pork and that she had better go back to the farm. And she does just what he tells her to do and blows in on the next steamer with busted purse, busted heart, busted liver and Texas tears all running down her cheeks. But you dare not censure her "dear duke"—she will defend him at the point of her—hatpin. Well, she has done the best she could; for the reason that she couldn't do any better. As good a reason as that for which a cow slobbers. It's because she can't spit. I'll ask you another question: Do you know why a hen sets? You know a hen will set on a dozen eggs, or on one egg; she will set on a good egg, a bad egg or a door-knob. A hen is often a victim of misplaced confidence. Why does she persist in her setting spells? It's because she has fever in her blood and she can't help it. And the way to cure a setting hen is to pump cold water on her back. Girls, whenever you feel the foreign lordship fever coming on, bribe your father's coachman to hold you under the town pump.

I will now give you my definition for a king and a traitor: A traitor is one who is not what he seems; a king is one who seems what he really is.

To illustrate, I will briefly relate to you the strange case of Dr. Jekyll and Mr. Hyde. The story is not a new one. It is the story of the dual life of Dr. Jekyll, of London. Dr. Jekyll was a philanthropist and a scientist. As an epitaph to his memory, he left behind him many monuments of noble deeds and virtue and valor; he became famous for his philanthropy, and the city loved him. He became famous for his discoveries in sience, also. Among his last discoveries was that of a strange drug, the ingredients of which were known only to himself, and which secret died with him, which drug, taken into the system, would distort the body, transform the features, steal away all sense of moral obligation and create a morbid thirst for blood; it would transform the man from his humanity into a shriveled, snarling, vicious monster.

After a few cautious experiments with his new discovery, Dr. Jekyll became emboldened, and purchasing all of the drug there was in the London market, he compounded a secret antidote, which counter-drug, taken while under the influence of the drug first mentioned, would recreate the fiend into his original humanity.

Dr. Jekyll now rented a flat in a distant and criminal portion of the city, and becoming established, announced himself as Mr. Hyde, the scientist. However, he did not abandon his actual home, but continued to dwell there most of the time. Thus began the dual life of this strange man, at home as Dr. Jekyll, the philanthropist; and in the new quarter as Mr. Hyde, the scientist. Here it was that he carried on those strange experiments with his new drug. Every night, measuring out a quantity of each drug, the latter to be taken upon his return after a midnight excursion, which was always just before daylight the next morning, he would disguise his clothing, take a heavy staff in his hand, and, swallowing drug number one—which would immediately, with convulsions and much pain, transform him into a snarling, shriveled monster, with the instincts of a murderer—he would dart through a rear door into the darkness, down an alley and disappear toward the ill-lighted portion of the great city.

Just at this time there were many murders being reported to the London police; the bodies were found mutilated beyond recognition, with throat cut from ear to ear and the heart plucked out and left mockingly upon the breast of the victim. The nearest approach to the solution of these strange murders was the appearance every night at about midnight of a strange, distorted form, half man, half beast, scampering wildly across the common, but which person or thing always skilfully eluded the police.

After some months, a detective more daring than the rest, discovered this person or thing in the act of accosting an unarmed man by the side of a tall, dark building. The fiend was chattering weirdly to his victim, and, chuckling over the morsel he was about to swallow, struck him a heavy blow with his staff and killed him. As he stooped over the form to further mutilate the fallen victim, the officer sprang at him—he was gone—the officer in pursuit; he followed him to his lair, and there, to his surprise, he discovered that he was none other than Mr.

Hyde, the pretending scientist. Mr. Hyde was so overcome at the thought of being discovered that he did not notice the officer enter behind him. Rushing into his laboratory, he threw open the doors to his cupboard to take from it the counter-drug which was to recreate him into his original humanity; but he threw up his hands in horror upon discovering that the drug was exhausted; there was not a grain left, and Dr. Jekyll was the only man in all the world who could make it. And in the frenzy of despair at his lost condition, he dashed wildly from one room to another, crying, sobbing like a lost child, biting his finger nails; and seeing his father's picture upon the table, leaped where it was, seized it in his claw-like fingers, tore it into shreds, threw it upon the floor, stamped it with his feet; and, tearing his hair, foaming at the mouth, he fell dead at the feet of the officer.

Dr. Jekyll was Mr. Hyde, and Mr. Hyde was Dr. Jekyll; two names, but the same person; two appetites, two characters, but the same personality; a philanthropist and a murderer, but the same man.

The inference from this strange bit of fiction is that of the dual natures in man. I believe that every man has a dual nature, that in every pound of flesh and every flame of life, from the animal down to the plant, there is a germ of good which draws upward, and a germ of evil which draws downward. You have noticed that a garden left uncultivated soon grows to weeds; a fruit tree of the finest variety, left unpruned, runs to scrubby fruit; and cattle of the finest strain of blood, left unassorted, terminate in stunted stock; and there is in man a latent force, which, with a maniacal grasp, seems to drag him downward to the gutter.

It is the Dr. Jekyll and the Mr. Hyde. The Jekyll draws him upward, the Hyde draws him downward; the Jekyll makes of him a philanthropist, the Hyde makes of him an anarchist ; the Jekyll makes of him a man, the Hyde makes of him a murderer. Some listen to the noble warnings of Dr. Jekyll; many listen to the whisperings of Mr. Hyde, forgetting that in so doing they are placing their heads beneath the millstones of destruction, the stones that will grind them to powder.

When Martin Luther was caught in a terrific storm of rain and lightning upon the highway in Germany, he heard two voices calling him, one to the right, the other to the left. Luther listened only to the Jekyll voice, and taking the path to the right, he found the Christ.

It was the Jekyll in Henry Clay that made him say: "I would rather be right than President."

The Mr. Hyde got hold of King David, and

made him commit adultery and murder; but, thanks
be to heaven, David had enough sense left to take
the counter-drug, repentance, and king David became what God always intended him to be, a man
after God's own heart.

Victor Hugo wrote the "Hunchback of Notre
Dame." Quasimodo, who is the bell-ringer of the
Cathedral of Notre Dame, steals the little helpless
dancing girl, La Esmeralde, from the streets of
Paris, and is himself taken by the police; that was
the Mr. Hyde in Quasimodo But the Dr. Jekyll
shows himself in even the Hunchback of Notre
Dame, when he afterwards rescues that same helpless dancing girl from the lascivious clutch of the
foul Priest of Notre Dame, Claude Frollo. The
Jekyll and Hyde together again.

But these men saw to it that the nature which
predominated was the Jekyll and not the Hyde. So
must you see to it that the nature which predomi-
nates, which has you last, is the Jekyll and not the
Hyde. You must check the Hyde at once, kill him
in the shell, or the Hyde encouraged will lull the
Jekyll to sleep forever.

It is the Hyde encouraged which makes men
steal, and rob, and betray and kill. It was the Hyde
in the president of a great savings bank that made
him rob the bank the other day, and that made him

sit at his desk and laugh at a feeble old woman who rapped timidly on the bolted door, and begged piteously for her fifty-five dollars—all she had in the world.

It is the Hyde encouraged which makes the husband false to his wife, the wife to her husband; that makes the clerk rob his employer; that makes the pretending Christian rob his Lord of his tithe; that makes the counterfeit Christian.

But the worst Hyde of them all is the suicidal Hyde. While on a lecturing tour in Colorado recently I purchased in the city of Denver a copy of Robert G. Ingersoll's late booklet, "Is Suicide a Sin?" I bought it for two reasons; first, to give the lonely infidel another chance to shake my faith; and secondly, to see if the Colonel is still as big a fool as he used to be. You know that he used to try to show us the mistakes of Moses; but the mistakes of Ingersoll so blinded our vision that we couldn't get even a glimpse of the old patriarch. For years he has been trying to convince us that we are agnostics, by telling us why he is an agnostic. And he has spent a lifetime telling us that Pope and Tom Paine were good men: while Pope and Tom Paine, both of them, on their death-beds, told us that they were going to hell. So when I read this book, this was my conclusion: That it is impossible for

Robert G. Ingersoll to be as big a fool as he seems, or to seem as big a fool as he really is. This is his logic: Because Sampson and Saul and Aristides and Aristotle and Nero and Antony and Brutus and Cleanthes and Sappho and Cleopatra—and a host of others committed suicide, therefore suicide is justifiable and is not a sin.

Is that logic? Then it is no sin for me to steal: for Jean Valjean stole the silver communion chalice from the bishop's holy sanctum. Then it is no sin for me to kill: for did not the noble Brutus stab the mighty Caesar? Then it is no sin for me, or any man, to ruin the fair name of Ingersoll's only daughter: for did not King David betray Bathsheba? Suicide not a sin? He knows it is, and he is afraid to do it himself. I tell you that the man who scribbles a hurried note, stating that he can no longer bear up under the slings and arrows of misfortune and goes and drowns himself, leaving his wife and child to bear up under those same slings and arrows of misfortune, is a coward and a poltroon. I don't believe the devil himself will trust him after he arrives below. I warn you, if any of you run across him after death to keep your eye on him—he will be Mr. Hyde down there just the same.

This, then, is the keynote of this lecture: Be what you seem; or else seem what you really are.

The cloak of Dr. Jekyll covers many a Mr. Hyde; and often there is lurking about the lips that whisper loyalty the kiss of betrayal; and many a hand which has dipped into the bowl of hospitality has afterward pressed down upon the head of its benefactor a crown of thorns. Be what you seem, or else seem what you really are. The monument of Absalom told the world that he was a good man and an upright judge. But that is what Absalom said of himself; he erected that monument with his own hand. The evil which lived after him was his true epitaph, and it told the world that he was a thief and a traitor, and that he even tried to kill his own father.

I love to look upon old things, old manuscripts, old books, old relics. There is something about them so time-tried, so true, so genuine. A new thing may change to-morrow; but a relic tried with a hundred years of time and still unchanged, is just what it pretended to be. In Colorado a few months ago I saw some Indian corn which had been taken from the home of the ancient cliff-dwellers, far up in the Grand Canon of the Colorado. The Pueblo Indians say that their father's father had no tradition, even, about those ancient people, so long have they been extinct. And yet that corn, lying in an earthen vessel in a niche far up in that cliff-dwell-er's home, hidden for hundreds of years, was just as natural the day I saw it as if gathered fresh from your fields but yesterday.

Once I looked upon an Egyptian mummy. The fine linen bandages around the body were printed, in indelible ink, with Egyptian characters, which declared that the death of that man occurred four thousand years before. In that mummy I saw a man who had lived in the time of King Pharaoh the great; who had talked with the contemporaries of the king; and perhaps had witnessed Moses and the children of Israel in their flight from Egyptian bondage across the Red Sea. Yet through that test of four thousand years of time the face and the features of that mummy had remained unchanged and true to nature.

That relic recalls the Pyramids of Egypt. They are so old that even Moses, in the traditions which he read, found no mention of them, so common they were as to be unworthy of mention. And yet the great granite stairways and partitions of those pyramids have not changed nor been racked so much as the distance of a hair's breadth in all of those four thousand years.

Look into a kaleidoscope. As you revolve its cylinder, its fifty bits of colored glass change their positions and fall into a thousand different figures;

it is a constant change, a delusion, a deception, and cannot be relied upon as can the corn or the mummy or the pyramid.

Again, I looked upon a chameleon; and every time it changed its position or moved a muscle its color changed; now a purple, now a green, now the hideous streaks of a serpent. And I said, I'd rather be an ugly toad, with mud upon my back, than to be distinguished by the deceitful effrontery of a chameleon.

Now, which are you—the old reliable pyramid, or the changeable kaleidoscope? Is your color the spotless white, or is it the streaks of the chameleon? Are you Dr. Jekyll, or Mr. Hyde?

I have heard that the way to put the Jekyll into a man is for him to marry. I don't know about that; but I do know that that is the quickest way to take the hide out of him. I have seen men who never amounted to anything until they married. Benjamin Franklin is an example. He amounted to nothing until he married; but he had not been married six weeks until he discovered chained lightning. Marriage does broaden a man; the second time it broadens him more, and the third time it flattens him clear out. In a cafe in New Orleans recently, there sat at my table a gentleman of quiet, sober, pensive demeanor. One day I ventured to break the silence; this is the conversation which ensued:

"Ahem! you are apparently a man of experience; you are a married man, are you?"

"Ugh! A married man? Experience? Sir, I've been married three times. My first wife was rich; my second was beautiful; my third was red-headed· Experience? I, sir, have tasted of the world, the flesh and the devil!"

Perhaps the dread of this experience is the reason so many men remain single. They might regret it. I recently found a couple in Chicago who did. I was stopping with a friend who lives in a flat. Now, the partitions in a Chicago flat are very thin, about as thin as Chicago religion. On the other side of this screen lived a young married couple; they had gone about six weeks. We heard them laugh, and we heard them quarrel; but we stood it all with an humble shrug, for patience is the badge of all our bachelor tribe. At last the crisis came. This Romeo and Juliet did stab each other with tongues of fire. Said Romeo: "I know what I wish; I wish I was single again." Said Juliet: "You do, do you? I did first. That's where you belong. Do you know that nine-tenths of the convicts in Joliet penitentiary are single men?" Said Romeo (O Romeo, how could you, Romeo!): "Which plainly goes to

show, that nine-tenths of the convicts in Joliet penitentiary prefer prison life to marriage."

Well, adversity will come sooner or later to every
man, whether married or single; sooner if married. I
once heard of a man who was happy; he married; then
he died. His wife pestered him all of his married
days, and even after he lay silent, defenseless in the
coffin, she followed him to his grave. Their names
were John and Mary; the woman's name was Mary.
Soon she missed. John; there was no more to be
heard that familiar ring of the door-bell at unfa-
miliar hours; there was no more to be heard that
familiar snoring sound from the other pillow; there
was no more—in short, there was no more John.
Mary grew lonesome, despondent; she went to a
spiritualist; she asked him to call up John. The
spiritualist rapped once on the outside of the chest;
a rap answered from within; two more raps were
answered, then three, then a fluttering of wings, and
Mary had the connection. This followed:

"Is that you, John?"

"Yes, Mary; what is it?"

"O John, are you happy, John?"

"Yes, Mary, happy."

"Are you very happy, John?"

"Yes, Mary, very."

"Are you happier than you were with me, John?"

"Yes, Mary, happier."

"O John—boo hoo—John, are you very much happier?"

"Yes, Mary, much happier."

"Where are you, John?"

"In hell, Mary."

However, do not let this trifling incident hinder you from marrying. Girls, I say marry. If a good man, reasonably sane, comes along and tells you that he is dying to have you get in and ride with him through life, get in; get in, but don't take up all the seat; ay, there's the rub that makes man grumble. I believe in woman taking time by the forelock, but not her husband. And young man, you with the wagon, two words of advice: Beware of the red-headed girl, and beware of the mother-in-law—marry one at a time. Often the mother-in-law fears the girl will not weigh out, and she goes along to make up for shrinkage. If she does in your case, and it at last resolves itself into the question, whether you are to let her have her way, or shoot yourself, don't hesitate a minute; shoot her at once.

———————

Lastly, I will speak of the demand for Kings. The world is in need of kings to-day as much as in the day of the rejected Saul. In all ages of social and religious development, leaders have been a necessity. In the thirteenth century, Luther dared to stand alone and aloft above his opponents to proclaim religious liberty and freedom of conscience. And in that, Luther became a king.

George Washington led the American army in the Revolution without salary or hope of reward; his only motive was Patriotism and Independence. And in that, George Washington became a king.

Abraham Lincoln, while still a young man, vowed that he would not close his lips in silence until the black man was made free. And though he died a martyr to that resolution, he himself fulfilled it. And in that death he became a king.

We need more Kings; not Sauls, or Napoleons; but more Davids, more Luthers, more Lincolns. We need Kings in Finance, in State, and in the Church.

We need Kings in finance, in the business world; men who will not only make their pound yield honest pounds, but who have the cause of Christ at heart in the use of those pounds. For the wealth of the world is not ours; the gold and the silver, the cattle upon the thousand hills belong to the Lord. We are but tenants here. And we are not even renters; we are but cropping; for the Lord has furnished the soil, the seed, the power (heat and rain from heaven); but, alas, it must be said that many of his renters are running away with the rent. For why are not all of the church debts paid? Why have not all the heathen the Gospel? Why are not all the poor cared for? Because the Lord is being robbed of His tenth. Where are your Kings in finance?

We need kings in state, in government. Men who will not sell and mart their offices for gold and patronage. Millions of the government's money go that way in every Congress. Where are your kings in government?

Most of all, we need kings in the church. Many churches are at a standstill; and it is not all the fault of the pastor. He may be a very bad man, often is; but I think it is because of the company he is compelled to keep. When you are looking for the faults in the church, stop just before you reach the pulpit—in your own pew. Many members refuse, not only to lead, but to be led; they are all the time pulling back on the halter. The regret I have is, that those persons do not get the halter around their necks. They would not be missed. The Lord would raise up a David in the track of each. Give us more kings in the church.

Every man and every woman may be a queen and a king. There are crowns awaiting in every avocation; in finance, in church, in state, in the trades, in the professions, in the sciences, in the arts. And every one is eligible; you do not have to be born a king; you need not come of royal blood; kings have been made of the common people.

David, with a shepherd's crook, was anointed king.

John Bunyan was a tinker, yet he became a king in literature.

The boy Shakespeare was worthless in Stratford upon Avon, but in kicking him out they kicked him toward London, and in London he became the king of poets.

Edwin Booth, at twenty-two was a failure but he persevered, and at forty became the king of actors.

U. S. Grant was a failure both at the bench, and on the farm—he could not raise beans; but he could raise a musket, and they sent him to war; and in war he became a king.

Henry Ward Beecher once almost gave up the ministry as a failure; but his good wife encouraged him, and, by the grace of God, he became the king of preachers.

And I cannot forget that other King, the lowly Jesus, born in a stable and laid in a manger. He was from the common people, a common man. Recently in the city of Chicago I saw the linen sheet on which Abraham Lincoln lay when he died, pierced by an assassin's bullet. It was saturated

with his blood. Instinctively I thought of the blood
of that other King. In His death He had no pillow
to His head and no cushion to His back; His rest-
ing place was the rough, unhewed timbers of the
cross; His covering was a crown of thorns, and vin-
egar was His drink, and in shame He died. Yet, in
that death He became a king, THE King, the King
of the world, the Messiah of God!

These were the accepted Davids. There have
been many rejected Sauls. There was "Jeroboam
who made Israel to sin;" and Omri; and Ahab and
Jezebel, that wicked pair whom the dogs ate in the
streets of Jezreel; and Herod who slew the babes of
Bethlehem. And there was yet another, the im-
perious Napoleon Bonaparte. It is said that, when
he was being laid in his grave, an exile, upon the
island of St. Helena, the heavens thundered and the
lightnings raged; and that nineteen years afterward,
when his body was being exhumed for removal to
its marble sarcophagus in Paris, again the heavens
thundered and the lightning raged and the waves
dashed upon the rocks, as if in eternal mockery and
condemnation of the king who had been rejected by
God and cursed by man.

Be a King. Be a David, a Lincoln, a Daniel, a
Peter, a Paul. Be a King in finance, in society, in

the church, in the kingdom of God. There is where you win the crown that will not perish.

The empire boasts its temporal kingship, its throne, its king and his glory. And it forgets the common equality of man; that, as dies the beggar, so dies the king, and then none is so poor to do him reverence. It was said of one:

"He was a king; but now *he*
Sleeps in the general all-lodging house."

And the cook who served him with wine and with onions reclines at his royal side; and the beggar, who trudged grudgingly behind his carriage and cursed his quality, now lies at his head, an uninvited guest, yet nevertheless an eternal companion. But whether in this brotherhood they have all been elevated to kingship, or all leveled to beggary, it matters not; for the beggar in death becomes a king, and sleeps as easy as his lord; and the king sinks into the caste of the beggar, and like him, is too poor to wear shoes upon his tired feet. The beggar and the cook and the king, all "fat themselves for maggots. And the beggar may fish with the worm that hath eat of the king, and eat of the fish that hath fed of that worm. And thus may a king go a progress through the guts of a beggar."

King Richard II. said that there is no glory in a temporal crown. He said:

"Within the hollow crown
That rounds the mortal temples of a king
Keeps Death his court, and there the antic sits,
Scoffing his state, grinning at his pomp,
Allowing him a breath, a little scene
To monarchize, be feared and kill with looks,
Thus infusing him with self and vain conceit,
As if this flesh which walls about our lives
Were brass impregnable; and, humored thus,
He comes at last, and with a little pin
Bores through his castle wall, and farewell king!"

But aim you at the crown that will not perish, and which, dying, you will not leave behind. It is not of gold. or of silver, or houses, or lands; not of fame nor fortune, silks nor wine:

"Gie fools their silks, and knaves their wine,
  A man's a man for a' that;
The honest man, tho' e'er sae poor,
  Is King o' men for a' that."

'Tis not the geld that makes the ring,
'Tis not the crown that makes the king;
For steel will make the strongest ring,
And Truth will make the strongest king.

www.ingramcontent.com/pod-product-compliance
Lightning Source LLC
Chambersburg PA
CBHW021442090426
42739CB00009B/1607